To. Mary Jo
Just Jes
need — Love in ———,
Sarah

MW01531149

Just Jesus

Sarah Berthelson
no. 2

Sarah Berthelson

xulon PRESS

I lovingly dedicate this book to my precious grand-children: Parker, Hannah, Summer, Chase, Hope and Heather; to my daughter-in-laws, Brenda and Melissa, who love my sons unconditionally; to my pastor, Dr. Ray Newcomb, who has taught me so much through his biblical teachings; to my brothers and sisters in Christ at First Baptist Church, Millington, Tennessee.

Contents

‑◑〰‑

CHAPTER 1

Just Jesus

"Thy word is a lamp unto my feet, and a light unto my path." Psalms 119:105

After much prayer and others asking me to write more of my story after writing <u>He Guides My Path,</u> I will share again of how my God's grace has been sufficient through my years. I would like to share with young people and parents that regardless of what we face, God is there. Jesus is all that we need in this life. Daily, as we go about our duties, whether it is a child who is going to school or a grandparent taking care of a child, God will walk through the day with you.

I do not understand how people get through a day not knowing our Lord Jesus as their personal savior. The Bible is and has been a best seller for years yet we do not read it. In many homes it is placed on a shelf or maybe a coffee table for others to see. The Bible is a letter to each of us from our God above to teach us the way in which we should go.

He knows us better than we know ourselves. He certainly knows what is best for us. Do we ask Him on a daily basis what He would have us to do that day? Most often we have our own plans for our future. If we give our life to Him and ask Him to guide us, He will. He promised us that. I have learned that He does a much better job with planning my life than I do. He knows what is going to happen tomorrow and He has a perfect plan for my life. I will not know what He would have me to do if I do not ask Him to show me and then listen for His instructions.

As a grandmother now, I can look back and see that God was there all the time, through the life problems and the good times. He answered my prayers in His timing, not always in mine. I read this once and it stuck with me:

God Answers prayer
Not in the way I sought
Not in the way I thought He ought
But He answered them in the best way for me

Isn't that wonderful? He does answer our prayers. He knows what is best for me this day and He has a purpose for me as I go through the day. I want so much to find His purpose for my life. Each day I realize my time is running out to serve Him. Oh, how I want to know I got it right, just the way Jesus wanted me to.

The lives of my children and grandchildren are so different from what mine was. My grandchildren do not know that we did not used to have buttons to push on our cars to get the windows to go up or down. They do not understand that my parents never knew what a microwave or a computer was. They do not know that we did not have to worry about crime in the community where I grew up. We did not have a television until I was a senior in high school and the shows were clean, without any sex or foul language in them. If only that was the way it is today.

I am thankful for all the modern appliances that I now have. My mother washed our clothes on a scrub board. She never knew what central heat and air was all about. I am thankful that the young people today have the wonderful conveniences that they have. Do they appreciate them? I do not know the answer to that. I just see that they want more and more, never happy with what they have. Work is so important now for them to be able to have more stuff. Do their children suffer? Probably not, but so many parents work that children are home alone after school or in child care all day. In those olden days, as we so affectingly refer to them, we did not know what a day care was. Mama was home. She always had cookies or something when I got home from school. Sometimes it was a baked sweet potato. That was really good. Do the kids today know what that is? Most of them probably do not. The best thing parents can give their children is time. They grow up so fast and what memories are you making with them?

My prayer for my grandchildren is they will be taken to church by their parents and that they will learn God's word and know that He is with them all day long. I want them to know they need not fear, for God will walk with them through this day and the next. He has a special purpose just for them. He loves each one and wants them to serve Him daily. I love my children and grandchildren so very much, but I know Jesus loves them more. That is a whole lot of love. Every day I pray for their safety and that they will be in God's will. Just Jesus is enough and I hope they will always remember that. The crises will come as well as the jubilant times and He will be there watching over them. As grandparents, we are needed in this day and time to share Jesus and our life with our grandchildren. God bless you today as you pray for yours.

Just Jesus

The only thing that matters this very day
Is the one that I need to hear me pray

Just Jesus is the only one that can forgive my sin
That is the way that my prayer life began

Just Jesus loved me enough for me to have eternal life
That brings me much comfort as I kneel to pray
Knowing he cares what I have to say

Just Jesus can guide me and keep me safe
As I stroll through another day
Hoping not to make too many mistakes

Just Jesus is enough to turn the frown into a smile
When I think of the price he paid and is alive

Just Jesus can fill the emptiness that often comes my way
He holds my hand and comforts me through
my fears and dismay

Just Jesus Is ENOUGH

Sarah Berthelson

CHAPTER 2

He Sent Me Into The World

—⟨⊙⟩⟨⟩—

"Before I formed thee in the belly I knew thee"
Jeremiah 1:5a

My Jesus is faithful as He promised in His word. He saw fit many years ago to send a little baby girl into the Reid family. My parents thought that they already had the desires of their hearts. They had two boys and two girls, just in the order they had planned but their plan wasn't God's plan and along came a baby girl that they named Sarah Ruth. I am that baby girl and I know, without a doubt, that God had a plan for me. I learned at a very early age that all I needed was Jesus. Just Jesus was enough to get me through the good times and the bad.

My dear father was a farmer. He was a good man and an honest man. His word was his bond. My daddy worked hard for us to have food and clothing. He paid off his bills at the end of the harvest. I remember going with him to pay off the bills from the store where he charged what we needed all through the winter months. He bought everything from fertilizer for the crops to the flour for the biscuits on store credit. This store had everything we needed. Mr. Boone, the good man that owned the store, loved my daddy as a friend and knew he would get paid. Most of our food was home grown including the meat, eggs, and milk. One of my fond memories was going to the grist mill with my daddy with a load of corn and watching the man and machine turn our corn into corn meal. We always had milk and corn bread. That is still one of my favorite delicacies at night.

My mother helped in the fields, as did my siblings, and cooked us three meals a day. Our family loved each other. Everyone worked hard but me and that was the benefit of being the baby of the family. I called what I did picking cotton, when all I was really doing was taking a ride on my daddy's cotton sack.

Mama taught me scriptures as far back as I remember. Many times they were out of context but she got the message across to me. I knew what Hell was at a very early age. A subject that not many people talk about now, but I just knew I didn't want to go there. I knew there was a Jesus that loved me and if I loved Him and lived for Him that I would go to Heaven when I died. I wanted to do that. I can remember singing "come into my heart Lord Jesus, come in today, come in to stay, come into my heart Lord Jesus." I really meant that and I was only about 4 years old.

We went to Church on Sunday. We walked about two miles through the woods to catch a school bus that took us to Fair River Baptist Church, where my grandfather had served as a deacon decades before. Mr. Versie Nations owned the bus and that was his bus ministry way back then. He was a kind man and I loved him. The kids that went to Church with me also went to school with me. I just loved everybody. As I began to grow up and learn more about Jesus, I wanted to know for sure that I was going to Heaven. That summer we had a revival at our church, like we had every summer. Brother Horn was the pastor and a good friend to my family. He came to eat with us often. Mama always fixed a great meal and fried chicken. I always had to wait until the preacher got his share. I usually got the wings. I love the wings now. Well, at the revival, I can remember singing "Oh Why Not Tonight" and I just couldn't stand still. I walked down the aisle and publicly gave my life to the Lord Jesus Christ. I was later baptized in Fair River with about twenty-five others that had been saved during the revival.

Jesus Christ became my best friend at a very early age. I prayed about everything and learned the power of prayer very early. I knew Jesus was always listening to me. He was my best friend. I didn't have an imaginary friend as some children have. I had Jesus - Just Jesus.

We lived down a road where there was not much traffic, except for the mailman. I looked forward to seeing the mailman. Sometimes he would bring me cards with bird pictures on them. I loved that. I also thought that he brought babies to families and I asked him to bring me one. I can remember stepping up on the sideboard of his car; yes, the cars had those things, and asking him if he had any babies from Sears in his car. Well he never brought me a baby.

Mr. Mullins drove a grocery truck down our road about once a week and he did a little better with my wishes. He brought around eggs, salt, pepper, sugar, flour and candy. A piece of candy cost a nickel which I didn't have, unless my brother Dewey had come home from New Orleans where he worked on a street car. I thought he was rich. Mr. Mullins told me if I had two eggs when he came around he would give me a candy bar for the two eggs. I can remember sitting down at the chicken house waiting for those old hens to lay an egg so I could get my candy bar. It worked more often than not. How could I not love my Jesus who I had asked to make those old hens lay their eggs?

My sister Mary was the housekeeper in the family and wanted everything spotless, including me. She was the oldest sister and I loved her dearly, but thought she took cleanliness to the extreme, especially when it came to me taking a bath and washing my hair. When I was just a little girl, I had a black girlfriend, who I dearly loved. I wanted to be like her, so I go into the fireplace one day and began to paint myself with soot. I rubbed it into my scalp and all over my face and body. I thought I looked real good. Mary did not see any humor in this. There was a creek about a half-mile from our house and she grabbed my arm and dragged me to that creek. The sand that I loved to play in became my enemy that day. She scrubbed me with sand and washed me until I was red. That little trip to the creek has been in my head all these years. Maybe therapy would help with that. My God has a sense of humor, doesn't he?

I remember another experience with my big sister. I was in first grade and loved it, until one day my pretty older sister came to get me. I was thrilled to leave and thought of myself as very special, to have my sister catch my hand and lead me away. I had no idea where I was going until I went into a room and there stood this huge lady in a white dress. She took out this needle, gave it a shake and before I could say "Scat", it went into my little arm. I held my arm at least a week. My mother gave me loads of sympathy so I used my stricken arm for all it was worth. As I look back and think about me being the baby of this family, it is a neat thing. Mama just did not allow her baby to do much as far as chores go. The big children got to do them.

I look back on those times and realize what a peaceful existence I had. We did not have an air-conditioner and it got really hot in the summer. We just put all the windows in the house up. We never had any fear of anyone breaking in. Fiddle, everyone was welcome to come on in. We never locked the doors. I never knew of anyone running to the doctor to get a pill for anxiety either. My childhood was glorious, even as poor as we were. I just know God looked down one day and said "I need to put Sarah Ruth in the Reid family". Isn't that exciting how each of us has our own little roots? They are different and special. I wouldn't trade my family for anyone else's.

Young people were courteous, respectful and most of them loved the Lord and went to church. The worst thing that most young people did to be bad was to smoke a cigarette. Wiley, my dear brother was considered bad by his siblings. He wasn't bad, just mischievous. Would you believe he became a wonderful preacher and has served our Lord so faithfully? Anyway he thought I should smoke, so he wrapped up an old weed, which was called "rabbit tobacco", and he told me to suck up on it. It burned my tongue, mouth and throat. Needless to say, I wasn't a good smoker and never tried it again. Children only think of the moment they are in. That was a stupid moment on my part.

Mary had many suitors coming to see her that I remember well. There were times when she would have a date with one of her beaus and she would let me tag along with them. She would put me in the theater until it was time to go home. I loved that! That was certainly a different time when you could feel safe leaving a child in the movies without fear. I was not afraid, because I knew they would be back soon. Usually, there would be another friend or two there and we would sit together.

My other sister, Billie, had a time with me. I followed her and her best friend, Tiny Maxwell, all over the county. Tiny lived several miles away so Tiny and Billie had to walk to see each other. Mama would tell Billie to take me with her. I now know Mama just needed a break from me. One day Billie and Tiny got so fed up with my talking and bugging them that they locked me in a shed by Tiny's house. I really don't know how long they left me but I still remember how mad I was at them. I got even by telling Mama on them. When Billie was waiting for her dates, I would go into the yard and make up songs about the boy and would sing to the top of my voice about them. She was so worried that I would embarrass her and I know that oftentimes I did. What are little sisters for? This sharing with you makes me realize even more how much of an oneness was in our family. I cannot remember any one fussing at me about my antics. Maybe I have just blocked that out.

Billie married after graduating from high school and moved to New Orleans. I was familiar with New Orleans since I had two Uncles that lived there and my brother Dewey went to work there after he graduated from high school. New Orleans was only a couple hours away and I loved going to visit. I would stay a week or two at a time in the summer. I continued to be a pest but loved playing with the neighborhood kids. I have long forgotten their names but remember the fun things that we did.

My sisters were good to my parents and helped them in every way they could after they left home. There was such love for each other that none of us could wait until all would be together, if it were only for a week. So many families today do not stay close. The Bible teaches us to honor our parents, yet I see so much disobedience and lack of respect today.

"Hearken, my beloved brethren, Hath not God chosen the poor of this world rich in faith, and heirs of the kingdom which he hath promised to them that love him?" James 2:5

CHAPTER 3

He Protected Me

"There hath no temptation taken you but such as is common to man; but God is faithful, who will not suffer you to be tempted above that ye are able; but will with the temptation also make a way to escape, that ye may be able to bear it." 1 Cor. 10:13

As I began to grow up and was tempted to do things that Mama, Daddy, and Jesus would not be happy with, I had to search myself of who I was and what did I want to be. Oh my, I did a lot of things that I am ashamed of. Often times, I simply did not want to do what I was asked to do by my parents. I often sulked and would not talk to Mama. She ignored me. She did not sit down and say, "lets go shopping and I will buy you something pretty." Does that sound familiar? No, she just let me pout until I couldn't stand it any longer. The nice thing is when I decided I had enough and wanted to talk, she just started talking back as if nothing had happened. I do not remember ever being sassy to my mother or daddy but I pouted. This is NOT COOL in today's language.

On a day when Daddy was working in a field far from

the house, Mama said "We need to take your daddy some water". So off we went with the ice-cold water jug for Daddy. I was skipping along talking to Mama and she hit me right in the stomach, just back handed me good. I was shocked but saw this huge snake all coiled up ready to strike me. My mother had protected me. I did not see the snake that I was about to step on but she did. That was God's protection using my mama. My brother Dewey was once bitten by a cottonmouth water moccasin and to this day I am scared to death of a snake. Even a rubber one from the dollar store can make my heart beat very fast. By the way, my brave mama got a big stick and killed the snake.

When I first started to drive, my sister Mary taught me how to do it. I cleaned out a ditch or two. That is what Daddy called it. I was allowed to go to church on Sunday nights by myself. One particular night I was coming home from church and the car was just bouncing all over the road. I could hardly steer it. Finally I came to a friend's house and decided I had better stop because the car would hardly go. I was scared so I ran into the house and told this man, a deacon in our church, and his wife about my car. He goes out to check it out and discovers I had been driving on the rim of the wheel for several miles. There was no tire! He took me home and picked my daddy up to come back to get the car. Daddy never fussed at me and went to town the next day and bought a new tire. God protected me that night from fear and harm.

My siblings had left home to go their way. I was about fifteen years old and my daddy told me to go plant some seeds. He had plowed about six rows for the seeds to be planted in. I had watched him plant one seed at time, many times. He called me "Baby" and I didn't care for that in my teenage years but sure would like to hear him say it again. Anyway, he handed me a little brown bag with seeds in it and said "Baby, go plant these seeds. When you are finished, come back to the house," Well, they were very small seeds, so I went to the field and on the very first row, I put them in my hand and "zap!" went the seeds in about two feet of the first row. I went to the house. When my daddy called me Sarah Ruth, which was pronounced as one syllable in his Mississippi speech, I knew he was not happy with me. He said "Sarah Ruth what did you do with the seeds?" I don't know if I answered or not. I went in my bedroom, got on my bed, and cried all afternoon. My heart was broken because I had disappointed my daddy. I don't know what he did about the seeds. I guess he bought some more and planted them. I don't know why I put this under God's protection but I sure learned a lesson. Do what your daddy tells you to do and do it right. If you notice my parents didn't come running to me to get me in a better mood. They just left me alone to think it out. It worked!! It was a lesson I learned, to do what God would have me to do. Just Jesus was there even then.

There are many things that I often reflect on about my school years. Some are not so good or should I say I wasn't so good? I remember my first speech in public. My sixth grade teacher, Miss Minnie, asked me, or rather told me, to make a speech at the 4-H club rally. This was an annual event in our county. I mean, this was the big deal of the school year. All the county schools would come together on this particular Saturday. The girls in 4-H clubs would have on their little green shirts and skirts and I believe the boys wore khaki pants and a green shirt. Mama decided that I needed a pretty new pair of shoes if I was going to parade all over town and bought me a pair. We marched up one street and down the other enough times for me to go home with the biggest blisters on my feet you have ever seen. My shoes were not as pretty in my mind anymore. Of all the kids, especially older ones that could have made a speech, I was the one selected to make it. I rehearsed over and over with Miss Minnie telling me I was not saying the word 'success' right.

I made the speech in front of all those people. It went something like this. "I would like to thank each of you, especially Mr. Carlos Smith, for making our rally a success. As one of your youngest members, I would like to say we will make the best even better in Lincoln County." I flew off that platform with relief that it was over. I could see the pride in my mama and daddy's face as I finished. Maybe it was relief. I know I said "success" just like Miss Minnie had taught me.

I was not done for the day. I had to have a project that I was involved in. We had CHICKENS! I picked out a chicken and told Daddy I would take that one. Then Miss Craig, our county 4-H leader said "you also have to bring a rooster." I didn't have a rooster. I think we ate him one Sunday when all those people came home with us from church. Mr. Dunn who lived up the road from us had a rooster. I asked Mr. Dunn if I could borrow his rooster to show for the competition. He gladly said "sure my dear" and Daddy caught the rooster and away we went. They put my chicken and Mr. Dunn's rooster in a pen and placed my name on it. Oh, I was so proud. When I got through with my speech, Daddy, Mama and I rushed over to the judging of the poultry. I learned that day that chickens were poultry. I could see Miss Craig and two men looking so serious and putting ribbons on cages. Well my rooster was not pretty. He was very old and pitiful looking, with big bumps all over his feet. I was standing by my cage when I overheard Miss Craig say "Put a blue ribbon on it." I know I did not have the best project by any means. I think Miss Craig was happy that this little girl made the speech. I was the happiest girl in the county to have won first place with my chicken, my borrowed rooster and my very sore feet. Now was that God's protection? You better believe it. That old rooster didn't die nor did I faint when I made my speech. That was my first experience speaking in public. God was just getting me ready for the plans He had for me later in life.

One day in my early school years, a county nurse came to the school to check all the kids and I went home with a note. I had lazy eye blindness. I was given a patch to wear over the good eye to try and make my lazy eye stronger but I didn't like wearing it and took it off when I wasn't home. I guess I wouldn't have made a good pirate. After awhile they gave up on keeping it on me and I went through school being able to see with only one eye. Was God there? Wait and see.

There are many stories I can share about growing up and seeing God's protection in my life. Just Jesus was all that I needed. He loves the little children of the world. These stories are some of my favorite childhood stories.

I made it through high school without too much difficulty. I was not a perfect student but I sure had lots of fun. I loved everyone at school. My teachers were Christians and they watched after me. Miss Minnie and Mrs. Wells were the ones that I dearly loved but I was scared to death of them. I just knew if I lifted my head when I was suppose to be working on an assignment that I would get in trouble. You know something, I don't ever remember either one of them paddling or embarrassing a student in any way. Oh yes, students were paddled in that day. I never got a paddling at school but I was scared that I would get one if I did not obey. So why was I so scared? I think I just wanted to be approved of. I wanted my teachers to love me and to be proud of me.

I wanted to be a teacher every since the second grade. I loved Mrs. Allen who was my teacher and wanted to be just like her. I did not think I could go to college because my parents could not afford it. My sister Mary wanted me to go so she paid my first semester tuition at the nearby junior college. One day at college the reading teacher sent a note for me to come to her office. I was scared stiff and could not imagine what she wanted with me. She gave me an eye test and told me that I could get a scholarship. What a blessing!!

Due to my old blind eye, I receive a full scholarship for the remainder of my junior college and for two more years at the University of Southern Mississippi. My room, books, food, everything was paid in full. Is that a coincident? I don't think so. It was Just Jesus taking care of His little sheep. I mean little too. I wanted to be beautiful but I had to settle for average. I was skinny as could be and wore glasses. Glasses were not cool then. Skinny wasn't in either. Today the skinnier you are the better. Huh?

I made it through college and began teaching a fifth grade class in Meridian, Mississippi. I dearly loved teaching. I loved the children. We had devotion every day and prayed. Now I would be prosecuted but I was there in God's timing. Isn't He an awesome God? He knew me before I was born. He knew I would have a blind eye. He knew if he had made me to be a beauty queen that I would have so much pride, that I would not have been useful for Him. He knows what is best.

As I look back on those years, I see his faithfulness and protection for me in so many ways: the friends I met, the cars I rode in, the boys I dated and the stupid things that I did. Even when I jumped off the Black River Bridge on a dare, which wasn't a smart thing to do, He protected me. He allowed me to have a burst eardrum, which I surely deserved. I can see His protection in it all.

"Ye are of God, little Children, and have overcome them: because greater is he that is in you, than he that is in the world." 1 John 4:4

CHAPTER 4

Siblings Are A Blessing From God

—⟨◉⟩—

"Honor your father and your mother, that your days may be long upon the land which the Lord your God is giving you." Exodus 20:12

Siblings are a blessing and I am so thankful God placed me in the Reid home to be the little sister of George Dewey, Mary, Billie, and Wiley. Each, in their own way, have been a blessing to me and made an impact on my life. Hopefully, they can say the same about me.

There are some fond memories that I will share with you. Dewey bought a second hand car in New Orleans and proudly drove it home on his day off from work. I remember running out on the porch to see the new car along with Mama and Daddy. There was no car! Dewey had left the car out of gear. There was this big ditch down by the barn and when we looked, we could see the top of the car in that big ditch. I think Daddy pulled it out with a horse. Dewey brought so much joy into our lives. He was the first to laugh at himself with his antics.

I have shared about Mary but one of the funny things to me was she was engaged to my wonderful brother-in-law, Don, for six years. He had to have gotten tired of waiting on her. Mary was the Southern Bell who taught me manners and how to dress. She wanted me to look my best.

Billie married her George and lived in New Orleans. George was the comic in the family and had the biggest laugh you have ever heard. He was Mr. Hospitality. We loved going to visit them because we were treated royally. Now there is a story I want to share about Billie when she was young. For some reason Billie wanted to fly. Wiley, the mischievous one, told her to put a goose under each arm and jump out of the loft of our two-story barn. Then the geese would hold her up and she would fly. She sailed out the barn and hit the ground big time. Thankfully, neither Billie nor the geese were hurt. Billie has lived with this joke all these years.

Now I don't know where to start with Wiley. He was always in trouble of some kind. Not with Mama, she thought he could do no wrong. Well let me be the one to set the record straight. Daddy and Mama went to town one Saturday and left Wiley to shuck the corn for the animals. He locked me in the room with the corn and made me shuck corn while he rode off on a horse. He showed up just before our parents got home. Would you believe that God called him to be a preacher? I have to say, he has been a wonderful pastor and has served the Lord faithfully. He is so loved by the people that know him.

There are always things that families can find fault with. In our family we chose to find the good in each other. That is what we were taught. I am sure our parents are smiling down on their brood. Each one of their children has served our Lord Jesus with their spiritual gifts. God expects us to love one another. He placed each one in the family that He chose for us. Forgiveness is a must. Because of our differences, there will be disagreements. If you have broken relationships, you need to fix them before it is too late. It breaks my heart to see people that do not love and care for their family. I am thankful that my parents taught us to love each other. That was their blessing. We loved Jesus and each other.

"Beloved, if God so loved us, we ought also to love one another." I John 4:11

CHAPTER 5

My Prince Came Along

⟪◎⟫

"Live joyfully with the wife whom thou lovest all the days of the life of thy vanity, which he hath given thee under the sun, all the days of thy vanity."
Ecclesiastes 9:9a

When I was about sixteen years old and began to have crushes on all the boys that came along, I thought I had better pray about this subject. I began to pray for that special one that God had just for me. I dated in high school, college and in Meridian but I just could not find the one that I thought was meant for me. I dated one guy that I met who said he loved me but I didn't love him. He made lots of money and was a lot of fun but I didn't know if he was a Christian. He only went to church with me once.

One night, sitting at a drive-in kind of like Sonic, three guys drove up beside my roommate and me. One got out and came over and talked to us. The other two were snobbish or so we thought. They followed us home because they were in the military and were going the only way they knew to get back to the base, or so they said. The next day Gary, the talkative one from the night before, called to see if he could come over and bring a friend. I had my Saturday morning hair, probably twenty curlers in my hair, and no make-up. I didn't care because I was not interested in impressing anyone since I was dating a guy from my hometown.

I met my Prince that day but sure didn't think so then. George was from Montana. He was handsome and training to be a jet pilot. The thought of him being from Montana was scary since I am cold if it even gets down to sixty degrees. I couldn't see me living in cold Montana. None of that impressed me. Well, the handsome part wasn't bad. He started calling every day when I got home from school. He couldn't go off base during the week so we talked on the phone. I didn't want to be rude so I talked to him. Mama had taught me to be polite to everyone. Soon my principal said "Sarah you have a letter". It was from George. He called every day and wrote every day.

George and I were riding to a friend's house one afternoon and something that I cannot remember was said, and I said "I don't know what I am going to do with you." He said "Marry me". That got my attention, so I thought I needed to make sure he said, what I thought he had said. So I said "I don't know what I am going to do with you." George replied with "Marry me." This is a long story but a short romance, as we were married in my parent's living room four months later by my preacher brother, Wiley. We had to keep it a secret until George finished flight training. I thought that was a ridiculous rule. Mississippi girls are not good at keeping secrets especially when it comes to romance. I told my principal, my best friend, all my family, and my pastor. After we were married, I asked him why he called and kept me on the phone so long. He replied to keep anyone else from calling you. Well, it worked, my line was always busy.

A very interesting part of this romance is that George had prayed for his wife. It was quite a story of how he ended up in Meridian and met me right away. Only God could lead a guy from Montana to Mississippi to meet the one He had chosen to become his wife. There has never been a doubt in our minds that God did not intervene here. When I dreamed of the guy I wanted to marry it sure wasn't one from Montana. I never thought of being a military wife. I wanted to settle down and serve God in a little Church near my parents. God had other plans and they were perfect for me. There were times that I had thought God was calling me to be a missionary and He did but in His way, I became one in the military.

George had to leave and go back to Pensacola for more training so I wore my wedding ring on a chain around my neck. Of course it was not showing. I thought it was a cool thing to do. Remember, I was supposed to be keeping it a secret. After Pensacola he was sent to Kingsville, Texas for more training. My school was finally out and I rode a train to Kingsville to be with him. I will never forget what my sweet daddy said to his baby that day as we waited for the train. He said "Honey you belong to George now, so go and make him a good wife." Wouldn't it be nice if every father would do that? I think grown children need to fly the nest when they get married. That is what God's word teaches, to leave and cleave! (Gen 2:24) Sure you are to stay close to your parents and love them dearly but they are not to treat you as if you were a child any longer.

We were married four years and wanting a baby all four of those years. We adopted our first son, Ky. I am so thankful that young lady did not believe in abortion. What a wonderful gift she gave George and me! Six months later we were expecting our second son, Chad. Four years later our third son, Shay, came into our world. I thanked God for them and said to God "three is enough". I am so thankful for my precious sons: Ky, Chad and Shay. They brought us more joy as parents than we could have imagined as they grew up. Each one, in his own special way, loved and served our Lord Jesus.

George spent two tours in Vietnam. Chad was born during the first tour and was almost a year old when he met his dad. Shay was born during the second tour and was three months old when George came home to see him. The military life was not perfect but it was our life. Each one of us has our own special memories of those years. God protected my George through the military. I prayed often for that and He answered my prayers.

It was not easy to have my babies and George not to be there with me. I moved back to Brookhaven each time he left to be near my family. I remember the emergency room runs with one baby in my arms and two toddlers hanging on to my legs. I did it without fear or panic. God was there all the time.

The boys got used to their daddy getting orders and us having to move. They didn't mind the moving, although it was hard on them to leave their friends, school and church. Wherever we went we found a church right away. That was our support group. We became active in all areas of the church. Now the boys have fond memories of their travels. They loved going across the country to see their grandparents in Montana. A year on the island of Okinawa was an experience for all of us. They are pleased with the fact that they traveled a lot and were able to meet lots of people. George took them to see as many historic sites as possible.

George has been beyond my dreams as a perfect mate. He is so respectful, helpful, and caring. He is the best Christian I know. I can say that because I have lived with him longer than anyone else. He loves the Lord with all his heart. He serves Him faithfully at work, in the community and in our church. He has been a great role model for our sons. He does so much, for so many, and no one ever knows about it. He is a humble man. I saw many prideful men in the military. I never saw that in my George. In fact, when he was Commanding Officer of a unit, he did not want the boys to tell anyone. Oh they did drop their daddy's rank at times to get out of a jam, but when their dad found out, they were in trouble. They laugh about it now.

I was not a typical officer wife, either. I knew nothing about that life until we were married. Then I soon realized that it was expected for officers to not be friends with the enlisted. I didn't like that at all. It sure is not scriptural. Therefore we made friends at church and most of them were enlisted. They were our brothers and sisters in Christ. We were required to attend some of the Officer only functions and we did, but I felt so out of place at those things. God's word had taught me that we are all equal. I wanted all to see Jesus in me and they couldn't do that if I thought I was better than anyone.

"And do not be drunk with wine, in which is dissipation; but be filled with the Spirit," Ephesians 5:18

I hated for George to leave me even for a weekend or even worse for a year but there was something awesome about seeing him in his flight suit, getting into that big jet and flying away. It was a beautiful site, especially when he flew in formation with two more plans. He loved flying and he was a good pilot, so his fellow Marines told me. I was very proud of him and so were his sons. I remember the day my mother was visiting and she saw him fly away to Cuba with two other planes. She was so excited to get to see that.

He Knew I Needed You

As I sit here and think of the one I love
I know that God knew I needed you
Of all the loves that could have been in my life
He knew I needed you
Oh how kind you are to me every day
Not once have I worried that you would stray
You are the one that He sent to me
He knew that I needed you
When I am happy you are there to laugh with me
When I am sad you are there to cry with me
If I need help in any way you come running
Oh how precious you are as I think of my love
That carries me through each day given by God above
It isn't luck that I am so happy with you
By God's providence you came into my world
When you spoke of Him, I knew you were meant for me
He knew I needed you for the rest of my life
I am so thankful He chose me to be your wife
HE KNEW I NEEDED YOU!!

Sarah Berthelson

If our young people would go into their marriages today believing that God had ordained their marriage and get things in the right order in the home (God first, spouse second), there would be lot less divorce. It breaks my heart to see so many young women today being the head of the household. The men become submissive so they will not upset the wife. They want a Christian home but it is not in the order that God says in his word. I see men not taking the needed responsibility with the children. Children need and desire discipline. When it is done in the right manner, it is an act of love. Children need both parents to love and share with. My heart breaks for the single parents. As a military wife being left alone a lot, I can identify with them in a small way. Sometimes I wonder how they do all that is to be done. If they will let Him, just Jesus will get them through it.

"And they said, Believe on the Lord Jesus Christ, and thou shalt be saved, and thy house." Acts 16:31

"Train up a child in the way he should go; and when he is old, he will not depart from it." Proverbs 22:6

Just Jesus sent my loves into my life and He will do the same for you.

CHAPTER 6

He Was There Through The Trials

"Wait on the Lord; be of good courage, and He shall strengthen your heart: wait, I say, on the Lord." Psalms 27:14

There are those who think that Christians have no trials. I have had plenty of heartache, sickness and death to deal with. I do not go around with a frown on my face because of it. Many times my heart may be breaking, but no one knows. It was through the valleys that God was nearest and dearest to me and that is when I grew the most. He allows the trials so we can help others with their trials. I feel that is a ministry that He has placed me in because everyone hurts in some way. It may not be for the same reason, but we hurt just the same. Just Jesus walked with me. He is the only one that truly knew how I felt.

My wonderful parents died six months apart when I was in my thirties. I wanted so much for them to know my boys and for my boys to know and love them. That was not God's plan. We were stationed in Beaufort, South Carolina and I awoke one morning with this strange feeling that we should go see my parents. I called George at work and asked if he could take leave for a week. Ky and Chad were in school and it was not like me to take them out. George took the leave and we went to Mississippi for a week. We had so much fun with Daddy and Mama. He rode the boys on his bike and took them for walks to the pond. The day we were leaving, he told me he was having chest pains. I called Mary, who worked for his doctor, and she got him an appointment at 2 o'clock that afternoon. We left and when we got back to South Carolina late that night, Mary called and said "Daddy had a heart attack". He lived about three months but never was able to do anything, as a lot of his time was spent in the hospital. God sent me home to have that week with my daddy. Daddy died on June 4.

When he died, I stayed home with Mama a week while George and the boys went back to South Carolina. My mama was so sad. When I left, I told her to come to see us and that we would come back Thanksgiving, when the boys were out of school. Billie and her husband brought her to see us and they stayed a week. Mama tried to be herself and play with the boys but I could tell part of her was missing. She died November 9th. Wiley went to get Mama and take her to the doctor. She was standing and getting her chest X-rayed when she had a heart attack. I was substitute teaching at Ky's school when I was called to the Principals office. George and my good friend were there. George said "Your mother has died." I thought I was going to do the same. That was a gigantic trial but God's grace was sufficient. Just Jesus walked me through the grief. Three weeks later George's only sister died from Carbon Monoxide poisoning while in her car, in Montana. That year was a tough time but Just Jesus was more than enough.

My boys had their share of allergies and sicknesses, as all children do. Each of these times was heartache for me.

Chad was my accident-prone child. He was the one to get bitten by a dog or cut his hand badly on a seashell. He jumped off the table when he was 4 and had to have stitches in his chin. Shay had asthma and scared me half to death many times. There was always something going on with them. Many times their dad was not home, due to the military, but God was there all the time to go with me to the emergency room. Ky was the one that seemed to be the healthy one. Only once did he have to have stitches when he fell on a broken glass at school and cut his leg. Shay decided to show the kids at church he could jump farther down the stairs than anyone else. Mr. Martin came to the church training class I was in and said "the scream came from Shay". His dad took him to the emergency room and found out he had broken his leg. You know, being a parent is the most wonderful and rewarding job that a person can have, even with the many conflicts along the way.

I had Lyme disease, that lasted two years, and I thought I was going to die with that. I have had several surgeries through the years. I am presently trying to get over a case of shingles that seem to be lasting forever. This has caused depression often, dealing with the itching, burning and painful neuralgia. Most people do not know when I am depressed. Most of us suffer with it at one or more times in this life. I can now relate to others who have suffered with this terrible disease. One day none of this will matter. I know that all these things happen for a reason and can be used to glorify our God.

My son, Ky, died July 25, 1994. There is nothing like losing your child. Through it all, God has been with me. He has used everything I have been through, including this loss, for His glory. He tells us in His word that all things work together for good. This was not good but it can be used for good. I cannot tell you how many parents I have had the opportunity to witness to because they have lost a child.

George's daddy died May 25, two months before Ky's death. My brother Dewey died a year after Ky. We cannot predict what is going to come into our lives but God already knows. My Heavenly Father was there to count all my tears. That is how much He loves me.

"Thou art my hiding place; thou shalt preserve me from trouble; thou shalt compass me about with songs of deliverance." Psalms 32:7

"The Lord is my rock, and my fortress, and my deliverer; my God, my strength, in whom I will trust; my buckler, and the horn of my salvation, and my high tower." Psalms 18:2

MAKE THIS TRIAL A BLESSING

Make this trial a blessing I pray
Today as I sat and read your word
I found a verse that really made my day
My brethren, count it all joy when you fall
into various trials,
Knowing that the testing of your
Faith produces patience.
But let patience have its perfect work,
That you may be perfect and complete,
Lacking nothing. James 1:2-4
God I seek your blessing as I face this trail
Use it to teach me patience for other to see
Make this trial a blessing for me
To feel your presence that I need
Give me strength as I go through this day
That I will spend my time studying your word
Using this time of quietness to pray
Lord use this trial as a blessing
To teach me the lesson I need.

Sarah Berthelson

CHAPTER 7

He Gave Me The Desires Of My Heart

"But my God shall supply all your need according to his riches in glory by Christ Jesus." Philippians 4:19

God placed us in Millington, Tennessee, when George retired from the Marine Corps. I had prayed for a home with four bedrooms and a pantry for twenty years. After living in base housing for all those years, I knew my hearts desire was to have a bedroom for each boy and a pantry. We looked all over the county for a house to buy. Our boys were always with us looking. After God had closed many doors on houses we were interested in, a lady that worked with me as a volunteer at the Thrift Shop on base, said, "come and see my house, I may sell it to you." She lived in the same neighborhood as my niece and I had watched the house as it was being built. It was a beautiful two story house with a circular driveway. George, the boys and I stopped by one afternoon and as I walked in the door, I asked her if she had four bedrooms and a pantry. She said "yes". After walking through the house with her and her husband, I told George to "make the man an offer". Our offer was much less than the house was worth but all that we could afford. Her husband immediately said "no way". George thanked him, shook his hand and we left. The next morning about 6:30 the man called and told George he would take the offer. We serve a great and mighty God and He gives us the desires of our heart. He promises us that (Psalms 37:4). The house was more than I had ever expected. It was God's house in God's timing. Did I say it was on 2 acres, which was George's input to my prayer for a house?

George retired and we moved into our new home. There was one problem that we had not known about. The boys would have to go to a private school a couple of miles from our home. We did not have much money so private school seemed overwhelming. It was expensive to send all three to a private school. There were times that I did not know where the money was coming from. One afternoon I knelt and asked God for six hundred dollars that was due for tuition. I did not know where it was coming from but He did. That is a lot of money but not for God. Would you believe that we got a refund from our insurance company for six hundred dollars just a day before their tuition was due? Chad witnessed that miracle and never has forgotten it. I always prayed about everything. I was so grateful to our Lord Jesus that we could pay their tuition. He has met all of our needs, not all of our wants. I am now so thankful that I have not gotten everything I have asked for. He knows what is best.

Early in our marriage a doctor told me I could not have children. As I have already written, He gave me three, in his way and in his timing. God is in the miracle business!! My boys were the purpose for my life. I wanted to be with them, share with them, play with them, and enjoyed cooking for them as they grew into the men they are today. In my first book, He Guides My Path, I shared some of the heartaches and good times I have had with my boys.

As I share my stories with you, I pray that you will be compelled to pray for your every need and every desire. Pray often and about everything. God is listening. I pray about the little things, too. I pray for parking places, safety, my car and even the wrinkles on my face. As you can see, I pray for everything. Just Jesus is all that we need. If you do not have Him in your heart today, please ask Him to forgive you of your sins. Ask Him to come into your life and allow Him to be Lord of your life. He is anxiously waiting for you to do that. He loves you. He went to the cross for you and for me.

"Children's children are the crown of old men; and the glory of children are their fathers." Proverbs 17:6

"And all thy children shall be taught of the Lord; and great shall be the peace of thy children." Isaiah 54:13

CHAPTER 8

The Boys

—◦◦◦—

"For I will pour water upon him that is thirsty, and floods upon the dry ground: I will pour my spirit upon thy seed, and my blessing upon thy offspring."
Isaiah 44:3

Motherhood was such a blessing and I enjoyed my boys. Their growing up years was such a joy for me. After Shay started to school, I substituted in their schools to be near them. I knew and loved their friends. I knew their likes and dislikes from food to clothes and I tried to buy for them the things they wanted. It wasn't easy to spend quality time with each one individually but I gave it my best try. They talked about their fears, disappointments, and girlfriends with me. We had a good life. I remember when Shay left to go to college, the empty nest hit. I think I cried for a month. George and I went to the mall and he smiled and said ,"I am so happy to see you go to the ladies section instead of the boys." I had never thought about it before, that as a mother, I did go straight to their department to see if there was a bargain for my boys. We dressed them the best we could. We also took them to fine restaurants on occasions, just to expose them to a life beyond hamburgers and fries. Some of the nice places they still talk about. They enjoyed choosing what we would do on their birthday. That day it was their choice of where we would go eat. This was their special day and it became their special time.

When Chad was in the eighth grade, he came home one afternoon saddened that one of his classmates could not afford to dress like the other kids for their upcoming graduation program, where each boy was to wear a white shirt and navy blue pants. Chad and I went to the Navy Exchange, bought the shirt and pants, and took them to the young man's home. They had very little furniture and were in an old, run-down, rental house. I saw the compassion on my son's face that day and the happiness as we drove away. God allowed us to be His instrument in making a young boy happy. He stood with pride in his new clothes on graduation day. Chad was humbled by the fact he had helped this young man. He told no one what he had done. God got the glory and that was my prayer.

I often prayed for God to send someone into my life that was alone or needy so I could go visit, take food, run errands and to this day I have someone in my life to take care of. I would take the boys with me to visit the lonely, frail, homebound people that God had placed in my life. As a family, we prayed for God to send us children that had needs for Christmas. We would then take toys and candy to them. It was my boy's blessings to do that. Our family was blessed. Just Jesus is what we tried to teach them. It is a blessing to see them with their children going to church and serving our Lord.

Shay would give the shoes off his feet to the homeless. He enjoyed helping the kids that were less fortunate than he was. He read his Bible often and I could see that he leaned on Jesus in his tough times, as well as the good times. He went to a public school for high school. He loved drama and one of our friends that had been at the private school was now the drama teacher at Shay's high school. When Shay was in the sixth grade, he had been in a play that she directed. When she took a job with the county school for our area, that settled it, he wanted to go where she was. He was in several plays and did a good job in each of them. One thing that impressed his mom was he was not ashamed to wear t-shirts with spiritual messages on them. Everyone knew where he stood.

Each boy came to know the Lord Jesus as his Savior. Chad was only six years old and he accepted Jesus at a backyard Bible Club. Ky was ten and Shay was thirteen when they were saved. This was a desire of my heart for them to know and serve our Lord Jesus. My boys were not always the angels that I have sometimes portrayed them to be. Chad and Ky fought like cats and dogs at times. If a glass or something was broken, I never knew who did it. They would point at each other and say "he did it." What was a mother to do? Even though there was sibling rivalry, they had more fun than fights. Ky never wanted Chad out of his sight when they were young. When they became teenagers there was a different story. You go one way and I will go the other seemed to be their motto.

Now Shay was another story. He was the one that was not afraid of anything or anyone and would run off when we would go to a mall. Chad spent most of his time hunting Shay for us. Ky wouldn't look for him. These years hold lots of fond memories for all of us.

Chad met his wife at that private school. She was in his class. Brenda Cooper was a beautiful blonde cheerleader. She was a good student and a good Christian girl. I watched all the kids at school and could see in the sweet countenance on her face that she loved Jesus. Chad liked several girls but during his senior year he got the nerve to ask Brenda for a date. They began dating and then attended Mississippi State

University together. Four years after high school, they got married. He graduated with a master degree in biological engineering and she graduated with a master degree in elementary education. They now have three children and their love for each other is obvious. Their first child, Parker, was our first grandchild. What a thrill to become a grand-mother. He is very special. Then Summer and Heather entered their family. I am very proud of these children that God so graciously gave to us. I am thankful for Chad and Brenda being the parents that they are.

Shay was active in Church and his wife to be was right there but they did not meet until it was in God's timing. Melissa Mitchell, a beautiful brunette, came into his life after college. After several dates, Shay asked me what did I think of her and I told him that I loved her. I had not said that before about any of his girl friends. He proposed to Melissa and they married in four months. They have three children; Hannah was my first granddaughter and first girl in our family. Then Chase and Hope came into their family. Melissa has a degree in elementary education and Shay has his computer business. I am very proud of this little family that God gave to me. They are active in Church and good parents. What more could I ask for? God continues to give me the desires of my heart! It is a bit ironic that Brenda, Melissa and I all have degrees in elementary education. Is that a coincident or God's perfect will? We communicate very well. I love my daughter-in-laws and I think they like me. This is not bad for a woman who the doctors had told would not be able to conceive. There are twelve in our family now and what a blessing and fun time it is when we are together. Our grandchildren are such a delight. God even blessed my desire for girls in our grandchildren. I have four. Just Jesus is the one that I have leaned on.

I am so thankful for the men that Chad and Shay have become and the wonderful Christian wives that were sent to them in God's timing. I know my daughter-in-laws were His perfect plan. How grateful I am for each one.

My Boy's Role Model

Every child needs someone they can look up to
Not because of their height but what they do
Their dad was that and you can't go wrong with that
He taught them honesty, to work hard, to honor the Lord
He took them to church, he never sent them
A marine fighter pilot, that made them proud
But apart from the guy that flew the jet
There was their dad who loved them so
He taught them to fix their car
Make repairs around the house
They began with simple things, then they got bigger
So did the boys and now they are men
Honest, dependable, God fearing dads
Now their children have someone to look up to
There are patterns we learn and we learn so well
Be a good parent and your child will not fail.

Sarah Berthelson

CHAPTER 9

My Church Ministries

I beseech you therefore, brethren, by the mercies of God, that you present your bodies a living sacrifice, holy, acceptable to God, which is your reasonable service. And do not be conformed to this world, but be ye transformed by the renewing of your mind, that you may prove what is that good, and acceptable and perfect, will of God. Romans 12:1, 2

I have taught a Sunday school class since I was twenty-one years old. God gave me several positions in the church and I loved every one of them. Wherever we went with the military, I got active in the church. God has used me in several different areas of activity. Often, I taught where my boys were. I worked in the nursery when they were babies. That was not my favorite thing, but I felt obligated since my children were in there. He never asked me to do anything that He did not give me the courage to do it. Just Jesus was all that I needed.

Now, I teach a Sunday school class of ladies and they are my dearest friends. Some of them have been together for years. Teaching my Sunday school class is very rewarding. I feel so inadequate to teach smart, mature women, when most of them could do a much better job than I am doing. This is a Christ centered class. We love the Lord Jesus and serve him faithfully. Some of the ladies are group leaders and they take care of their group. All are wonderful prayer warriors, not only for our class but for our entire church family. Our class is bonded in a sisterhood. We love each other and know that we have someone when we need to laugh, cry or pray. We do a lot of that. They were my support group during my difficult times. When one is sick or loses a loved one, they know the rest are there for them. Several have become widows during the last few years. We have had three of our class members go to be with our Lord Jesus. They are missed but we know they are in Heaven. Everyone needs a good Sunday school class and church family. I love my class and my church family. Jesus knew just where to place me.

My Church ministry is so rewarding. I am a member of First Baptist Church, Millington, Tennessee. My pastor, Dr. Ray Newcomb is also a friend. He, his wife Carolyn, and son Brent are very dear to my family. He teaches God's word and I have learned so much from him the past twenty-five years. His mission is to lead souls to Christ. He does a great job of doing that. We are and have been very active in our church. The boys grew up with Brother Ray as their spiritual leader and that was a good thing for us as parents. I am thankful my boys had God's word taught to them at home and church. I suggest all parents get their children in a church where the word of God is preached. The church is not there just to entertain your children but to help us prepare them for the life ahead. We do our children a disservice if they are not involved in church. Take them to church and let them get to know our Lord Jesus and walk with Him.

God also gave me ministries outside my church family. There have been so many times that He has sent someone to my home that needed to talk. I have had ladies come that were not sure of their salvation. I have had many young women come that needed to talk to an older woman about whatever was on their mind. Most of them just need an ear to listen to their problems. I have had people call that I have never met because someone told them to call me about a problem. I feel so inadequate but God always gives me the words to say to comfort them. Jesus is the third person in all these conversations.

There was a time that I came into possession of a nice van while helping another family out of a financial crisis. It was an extra vehicle and I was not sure what I was going to do with it. This particular evening I took a prayer walk around my neighborhood. When I got home, a neighbor came to my door. As soon as I walked in, she said that she wanted me to tell her about Jesus. As I was witnessing to my neighbor, a young friend, who was a seminary student, his wife and four children were coming in another door. George talked to them while I did what I needed to do for my Jesus. After my neighbor left, we quickly fixed hot dogs for this family. My friend said "we need to talk to you." I had led his wife to the Lord several years before and they knew we loved them and would pray for them. When we cleaned up the kitchen, we went into the living room where this young man said "we need for you to pray for us." They had come from North Carolina and were going back in a couple of days. I knew it was a serious prayer request. He said "we are about to go on the mission field in Mexico and our greatest need yet unfulfilled is for a van for these children." I said "we have one in the front yard and you can have it." He couldn't believe it. He had no idea we had that van. I smiled because, that is just the way our Lord works. He knew all the time what I needed to do with that van.

When God gives you a gift or ability, He will give you the opportunity to use it for His glory. Remember my first speech when I was in the sixth grade? Through the years and in different churches, I have been asked to speak at women's luncheons, banquets and other gatherings. I have never been asked to make a speech that I was not nervous as could be, up until the time I stood up to talk. Then God takes over, calms me and I can talk, many times without looking at my outline. It has become a blessing to share with others what God had laid on my heart. I did speak to a ministers association in South Carolina but that is not something I enjoy. I just don't see where I have done anything that men can relate to. Everyone has a testimony and can be used by God to share it.

"Give, and it shall be given unto you; good measure, pressed down, and shaken together, and running over, shall men give into your bosom. For with the same measure that ye mete withal it shall be measured to you again." Luke 6:38

Someone Is Waiting

Someone is waiting for you to knock on their door.
Someone needs Jesus and that is what we are here for

To go into the highways and hedges, and find them.
For sure, they need Jesus and are waiting for you
To reach out and win them to our Jesus, this day.
Win them for Him. That is what He has to say.

Bring them in to church and train them to know more
About Jesus and our love for each one will show.
It is all about Jesus. This is the reason we go

Someone is waiting for that knock on the door.
He is speaking to you. So, please don't ignore.

Ask Him to deliver you from all of your fears.
You will feel His presence As you go near.

Someone is waiting for you to introduce them to Jesus,
this year.
Someone is waiting for you, and only you,
to knock on their door.

God is calling to you to go and win this lost soul
from the pit of sin.
You are all that He has to reach them; so go, reach, win,
train, and send.

May God bless you as you knock on the door.

Dedicated to Dr. Ray Newcomb,
Pastor of First Baptist Church, Millington, Tn.
His mission is to win souls to Christ

Sarah Berthelson

CHAPTER 10

God Gave Me A Worldwide Ministry

⟶⟩⟨⟵

"And he said unto them, Go ye into all the world, and preach the gospel to every creature." Mark 16: 15

The grief of losing my son was terrible but God was there all the time. One morning, I knelt to pray and I asked my Lord Jesus if he would give me something to do at home for Him. I just have this need to know that I am serving Him each day. The next morning to my great surprise, I woke up with these poems in my head. Oh yes, I know you have heard that before. Well it happened. I don't like poetry and certainly had never written any. My Shay had taught me some computer skills so I sat down at the computer and began to write poems. I wrote lots and lots of poetry. All of it came from my heart. I could not write about the bees or the trees, it had to come from my heart. I published three books of poetry and placed many more poems on the internet with God leading me. Many people have used them on their web pages. They always fix them up with fancy stationary and music sometimes but I cannot do pretty things like that. My computer skills are limited. I have met so many wonderful people from all over the world after God has shown them the way to a poem or two. I have even had pastors and staff members ask if they could use them. God is being glorified and He is the one that has sent them all over the world. Isn't God amazing?

Then one morning this wonderful man emailed me. He has a worldwide prayer ministry and asked if I would consider praying about becoming a prayer warrior for his organization. George and I prayed about it. For the past two years I have answered prayer requests from all over the world and people from every walk of life; ministers, missionaries, doctors, heartbroken parents, prisoners - people with all types of problems. You name it and I have heard it. I sincerely pray for and minister to these people. I had never realized how many people all over the world, and in every language, are hurting and need prayer. They need to tell someone their problems and know it is safe to tell me since I talk to nobody in their world. I have learned that I can be a soul winner on the internet. Many have written wanting to know how to know Jesus Christ. It is my blessing to minister to these people. People in very important positions from other countries have written for specific prayer needs. Some of them remain my email friends and we keep in touch. I don't know how it is done but my southern drawl is changed into their language and their language into mine somewhere in this prayer ministry.

This has been one of the most rewarding ministries I have had the privilege of serving in. I truly have learned to be careful what you ask for if you don't mean business when asking of our Lord Jesus. He amazes me in the answers and the scriptures that I need. Many times I have no idea on my own where to start with these people. I pray about what to say to them, and then the words and the scripture just come. It is Just Jesus helping me with this ministry that He led me to. I have made friendships with people in India, Africa, Asia and Europe that are keeping in touch weekly. If they have other prayer request they tell me. In all thy ways acknowledge Him and He will direct thy path. I certainly can testify to that.

"I can do all things through Christ which strengtheneth me." Philippians 4:13

"But ye shall receive power, after that the Holy Ghost is come upon you: and ye shall be witnesses unto me both in Jerusalem, and in all Judaea, and in Samaria, and unto the uttermost part of the earth." Acts 1:8

God's Holy Word

Today, I bought a new Bible,
Just because I wanted to.
I have worn out three or four.
Reading His word makes me want more.

I know the Bible is His inspired word.
It speaks to me like nothing I've heard.
He is there, just speaking to me.

Every verse speaks to me so clearly
That I know He spoke to me, dearly.
He loves me because He tells me so.

God is my Savior, my Friend, my Confidant.
I can tell Him anything and He listens.
All the little things, in my life, are important to Him.
That is the reason I pray, all day, to my Father.

He answers my prayers in such mysterious ways.
Most unexpectedly things fall in place.
He is so wonderful and gives me His grace.

God's Holy word is so precious to me,
Because He tells me what He wants me to be.
He sends me on ministry that I would not think of,
Because He loves me and asks me to serve Him.

Jesus asked His disciples to spread the word.
He asked me to do the same, in this old world.
I thank Him, today, for using a worm like me.
He can see a butterfly that will soon be.
Obedience is what He asks of me.

Sarah Berthelson

CHAPTER 11

God Loves Even Me

⟶⟡⟵

"For God so loved the world, that he gave his only begotten Son, that whosoever believeth in him should not perish, but have everlasting life." John 3:16

Over two thousand years ago my Father came into this world to save me. Because he did that, I will have everlasting life when this one is over. I will go to heaven and see my Savior face to face. I will be able to see my parents and loved ones again. The most important one, Just Jesus, will be there to welcome me home. In His word He tells me that He has gone to prepare a place for me that where He is, there I will be. Isn't that a wonderful promise to know?

God has given me a great life on this earth; everything that I needed and everything that I wished for. I would not change a thing. Being a poor farmer's daughter was such a blessing. I would not trade it for great riches. That old cold house I was born in and lived in until I was thirteen years old makes me appreciate this warm house that I now have. I didn't have a toy store to go to nor did I have the money to buy toys. I spent my days making dolls of rags or even an ear of corn, that daddy would pull off the stalk, would become a doll for a day. I often played like the clay on the side of a ditch was my "ice house" and I would pretend to chop ice for my playhouse. I had been to an icehouse with my daddy and saw them use an ice pick to pick off twenty-five pounds for my daddy. Kids do not have any reason to use their imagination today. You can buy everything they could dream of at the dollar store.

When my grandchildren come for a visit, Bebe, as I am affectingly called, takes them to the dollar store. It is just as much fun for me as it is for them. It is my blessing. They are my blessings. I want to make some good memories of their Bebe. Most importantly I want them to know that she loved the Lord Jesus with all her heart. That He was the most important one in her life. Her desire was to be used for Him. Bebe's prayer is that her grandchildren will grow up to be used by our Lord Jesus.

The brothers and sisters that He placed in my life are the best that I could have. Through them I have been blessed with many nieces and nephews, great nieces and nephews and even great-great nephews now. I love them all. My prayer for my friends and family is that they will get their focus off themselves and let God have first place in their lives. I have made so many mistakes in my life and as I look back it was for me that I did those things. 'If only', those two words are in my vocabulary often as I grow older but all the 'if only' cannot be redone. Just Jesus and His forgiveness is what I need.

As a senior citizen now, I hear so many people my age and older say "oh how I wish I had served God in my younger years". Dear ones, we have one chance at it. We can not turn back time. Many of you that read this book are looking to be entertained and to buy more today than you did yesterday. You cannot take one thing with you but your soul. What have you done with Jesus? Do you love Him? Have you placed Him first in your life, before anything else? Are you serving Him with your spiritual gifts? Ask yourself,

"What have I done for Jesus?" Only you can answer that. He wants all of you, your worship, your talents, your gifts. Give your life to Him today. Just Jesus is all that you need today and tomorrow. He loves even me and He loves you.

I pray that every person, that reads this book, will not wait until it is too late in his or her life to know Him. Many are acquainted with Jesus but do you KNOW Him? Talk to Him because you long to or walk with Him because you long for His presence. Do you read His word just because you want to know what He is saying to you this day? I pray God's blessings upon you my friends, my family and each person that reads this book. You can see that God has blessed this lady beyond measure.

Jesus, I Love you

Jesus, I love you and thank you for your love for me.
If it were not for your love, I could not get through the day.
That is the reason I kneel and pray,
"Jesus, I Love you."

You came into the world, to save me from sin.
You are my father, my Lord and my King.
I am so humbled by your love, I don't know where to begin
To tell you how much I love you

Thank you for getting me through this valley, today.
Pull me back up, on the mountain. I know I won't stay.
It is the valley where I call on you and pray,
"Jesus, I love you."

You are my friend, who rides with me in the car.
Everywhere I go, there is where you are.
I do not fear because you are there.
"Jesus, I love you."

When my heart is breaking and there are tears,
You lift me up and take away my fears.
God, I am so blessed to know you are there.
"Jesus, I love you."

Thank you for giving me a family that I love.
Because of you, I know, one day, I will fly like a dove;
To Heaven, where there will no heartbreak or tears.
"Jesus, I love you."

Sarah Berthelson

My Prayer for this second book is that my Lord Jesus Christ will be glorified and that you have received a blessing by seeing that God can use anyone for anything that He desires. "God doesn't need our ability, He wants our availability" as my Pastor has often said. May God bless you in a special way today! He has a perfect plan for your life. Do you know what it is? I sure never thought I would be writing books and he didn't give this to me until I was in my grandmother years. You never get to old to serve Him. When He is finished with you, He will take you home. Something to think about!

"Therefore if any man be in Christ, he is a new creature: old things are passed away; behold all things are become new. " 2 Corinthians 5:17

APPENDIX A

Jesus, Your Personal Savior

The Bible tells us how we can have a personal relationship with Jesus Christ and spend eternity in heaven with him. If you don't know that you will be spending eternity with Him, please read this to find out how you can.

The Bible tells us that God loves us and want us to be His children.

"This is love, not that we loved God but that He loved us..." 1 John 4:10

Sin separates us from God and all of us have sinned.

"For all have sinned and come short of the glory of God." Romans 3:23

"For the wages of sin is death, but the gift of God is eternal life through Jesus Christ our Lord." Romans 6:23

Under the Old Testament (pre-Jesus) law, a blood sacrifice was required in order for sin to be forgiven.

"For the life of the flesh is in the blood" Lev. 17:11

" . . . without shedding of blood is no remission(forgiveness of sin)" Hebrews 9:22

What can we do now to remove the sin that separates us from God?

Nothing, in ourselves, but He has already done something!!!

"For God so loved the world that He gave His only begotten Son that whosoever believes in Him should not perish, but have eternal life." John 3:16

"But God commendeth His love toward us, in that, while we were yet sinners, Christ died for us." Romans 5:8

Just Jesus! That's it! Jesus is the <u>only</u> way to God! Jesus died on the cross to pay the penalty for our sins. He paid the death penalty for us, so we don't have to. He was buried, rose from the dead, and now He has gone to prepare us a place in heaven. Heaven is His free gift to us.

This is all you have to do to accept this wonderful gift:

1) Realize that you are a sinner and because of that, you are condemned to death, which includes eternal separation from God in Hell (Romans 2:23 and 6:23, above)
2) Repent of your Sin (Be sorry you have sinned and try not to again)
3) Believe in Jesus and that he died in your place and rose again, paying the price required for the forgiveness of your sin (John 3:16)
4) Receive Jesus by praying and asking him to be Lord of your life

"If you confess with your mouth Jesus is Lord, and believe in your heart that God raised Him from the dead, you will be saved." Romans 10:9

5) Confess your faith and trust that Jesus will do what he said he will do

"If we confess our sins, He is faithful and just to forgive our sins, and to cleanse us from all unrighteousness" 1 John 1:9

If you would like to do that now, you can do that by simply praying a prayer like this one:

Dear God,

I know that I have sinned and that my sin separates me from you. I am sorry for that sin. I believe that you sent your son, Jesus, to die on the cross, in my place, so that my sin can be forgiven and I can live eternally with you. Lord Jesus, please forgive me and come into my life and be the Lord of my life. I will follow you the rest of my life. Thank you, Jesus, for saving me. Amen.

If you just prayed that prayer, then you are a newborn Christian, a new creature – a child of God, Himself!!! You will live forever with Him.

"But as many as received Him, to them gave He power to become the sons of God, even *to them that believe on His name"* John 1:12

"For whosoever shall call upon the name of the Lord shall be saved." Romans 10:13

Jesus will be there at all times, from now on. He will "never leave nor forsake you" (Hebrews 13:5).

You have a lot of growing to do. You should be baptized in obedience to the Lord Jesus Christ. This is a public testimony of your salvation. You need to quickly seek out and join a Bible-believing church led by a Bible-teaching Preacher and start praying, studying the Bible, and telling others what you've found.

"Be not thou therefore ashamed of the testimony of our Lord . . . ." 2 Timothy 1:8

Printed in the United States
36181LVS00002B/1-102